BY SLOANE GOULD

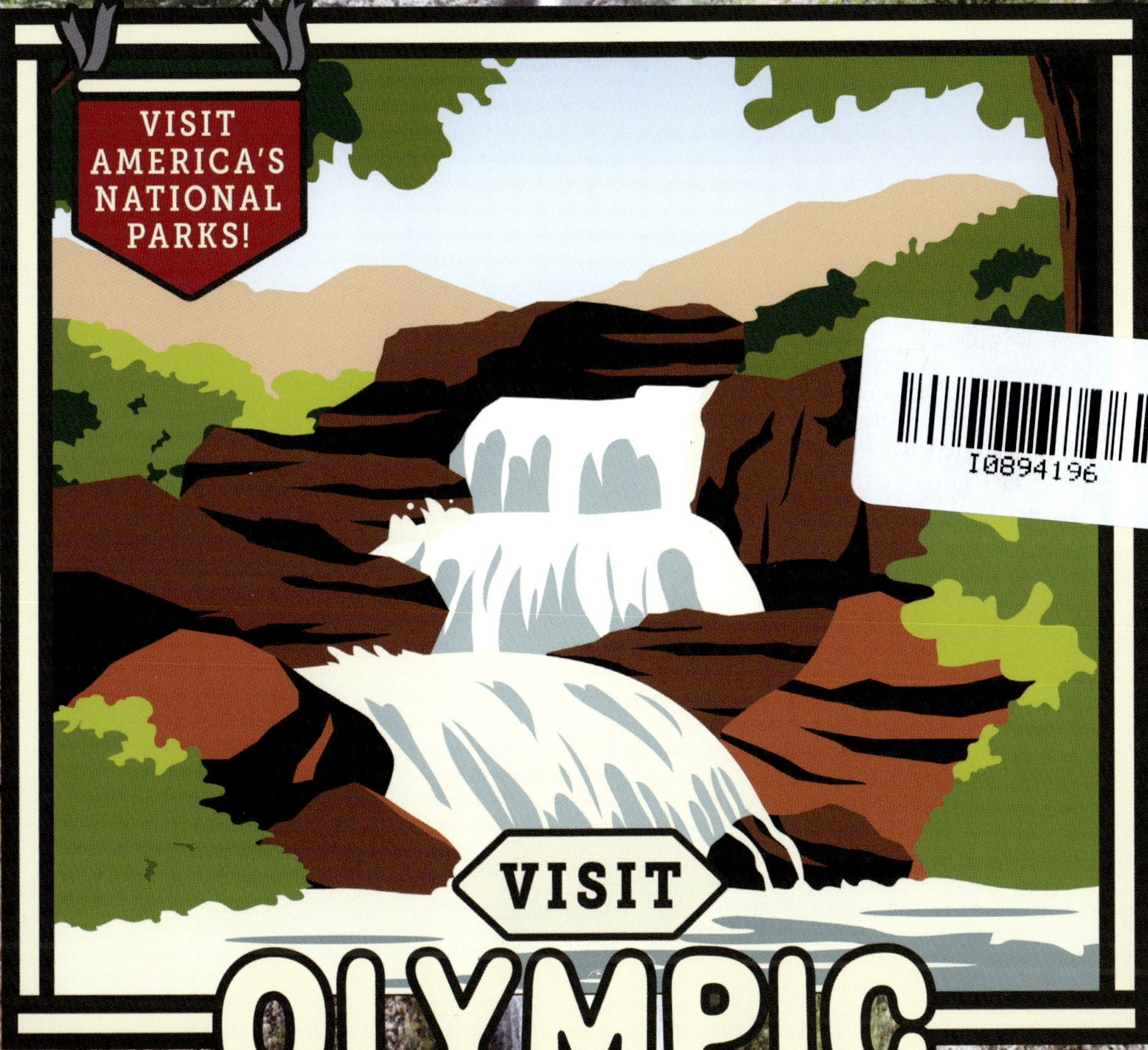

VISIT OLYMPIC NATIONAL PARK!

Enslow PUBLISHING

Please visit our website, www.enslow.com. For a free color catalog of all our high-quality books, call toll free 1-800-398-2504 or fax 1-877-980-4454.

Library of Congress Cataloging-in-Publication Data
Names: Gould, Sloane, author.
Title: Visit Olympic National Park! / Sloane Gould.
Description: Buffalo, NY : Enslow Publishing, 2026. | Series: Visit America's national parks! | Includes bibliographical references and index.
Identifiers: LCCN 2024058629 (print) | LCCN 2024058630 (ebook) | ISBN 9781978544222 (library binding) | ISBN 9781978544215 (paperback) | ISBN 9781978544239 (ebook)
Subjects: LCSH: Olympic National Park (Wash.)–Juvenile literature.
Classification: LCC F897.O5 G685 2026 (print) | LCC F897.O5 (ebook) | DDC 917.97/98–dc23/eng/20250130
LC record available at https://lccn.loc.gov/2024058629
LC ebook record available at https://lccn.loc.gov/2024058630

Published in 2026 by
Enslow Publishing
2544 Clinton Street
Buffalo, NY 14224

Designer: Tanya Dellaccio Keeney
Editor: Caitie McAneney

Photo credits: Cover (background) Galyna Andrushko/Shutterstock.com; cover (illustration) Butter Bites/Shutterstock.com; p. 5 jfergusonphotos/Shutterstock.com; p. 5 (bottom) Stacey Lynn Crary/Shutterstock.com; p. 6 https://upload.wikimedia.org/wikipedia/commons/1/18/These_large_canoes_are_hand_hewn_from_single_cedar_logs_by_the_Quillayute_%28Quileute%29_Indians_at_La_Push._This_canoe%2C_nearing_%284c29bba37af4487e83b8371c3df96873%29.jpg; p. 7 Michael J Magee/Shutterstock.com; p. 9 David B. Petersen/Shutterstock.com; p. 11 (top) Wirestock Creators/Shutterstock.com; p. 11 (bottom) Fotogro/Shutterstock.com; p. 13 Zack Frank/Shutterstock.com; p. 15 (top) Ellie Kaskey/Shutterstock.com; p. 15 (bottom) Tobin Akehurst/Shutterstock.com; p. 17 Jillian Sage Stetter/Shutterstock.com; p. 19 Francisco Blanco/Shutterstock.com; p. 21 (top) Anna Brzozowska/Shutterstock.com; p. 21 (bottom) RuchiImages/Shutterstock.com.

Printed in the United States of America

CPSIA compliance information: Batch #CSENS26: For further information contact Enslow Publishing at 1-800-398-2504.

CONTENTS

Words in the glossary appear in **bold** type the first time they are used in the text.

A PARK ON THE PACIFIC

The Pacific Northwest is a special part of the United States. It has a **rugged** coastline, sandy beaches, and tall mountains. It's also one of the only places in the United States that has a **temperate** rainforest.

Olympic National Park shows visitors the best of the Pacific Northwest. Animal lovers can spot whales and sea otters from the coast and marmots in the mountains. With almost a million acres of land, this national park is a great place to hike, surf, and camp.

Lake Crescent is one **attraction** in Olympic National Park.

MORE TO KNOW

More than 2.9 million people visited Olympic National Park in 2023.

A LONG HISTORY

People have lived in the area that is today Olympic National Park for thousands of years. Native groups include the Hoh, Quinault, and Skokomish. In the 1800s, more white settlers started to come to the area. To **protect** the trees there, President Grover Cleveland named it Olympic Forest **Reserve** in 1897.

In 1909, the reserve was made into Mount Olympus **National Monument** by President Theodore Roosevelt. In 1937, President Franklin Roosevelt made it a national park.

Native peoples often traveled by canoes, like this one, along the coasts of the Olympic **peninsula**.

MORE TO KNOW

President Theodore Roosevelt wanted to protect the land for a species, or kind, of elk that was suffering. It's now called the Roosevelt elk.

EXPLORING THE COAST

Set on a peninsula, Olympic National Park has 73 miles (117.5 km) of coastline on the Pacific Ocean. A large part of its coastline is made of rocky headlands. However, visitors can enjoy many sandy beaches, including Kalaloch Beach and Ruby Beach.

Rialto is a popular rocky beach. The view from Rialto Beach is one of the best in the park. Visitors can also explore the **tidepools** along the coast. Small creatures such as crabs, starfish, and clams live there.

One coastal spot in Olympic National Park is Second Beach.

MORE TO KNOW

A headland is a thin piece of land that juts into the ocean.

SPOTTING SEA STACKS

Sea stacks are big pieces of rock that stick out of the ocean. You can see many sea stacks along the coast in Olympic National Park. Some of the most popular spots to see a sea stack are Rialto Beach, Ruby Beach, and South Beach.

Sea stacks are made by **erosion**. Over many thousands of years, waves crash into headlands, wearing holes in them. These may form an arch at first. When the top crumbles, it makes a sea stack.

These sea stacks can be seen from Rialto Beach in Olympic National Park.

MORE TO KNOW

A mile-long stretch of sea stacks off Shi Shi beach is called Point of Arches.

RAINFOREST FEATURES

The temperate rainforest is one feature that sets Olympic National Park apart. People come to the park to explore the Hoh Rainforest, which is home to owls, bobcats, and elk.

The floor of the rainforest is covered in green mosses and ferns. Many different trees stand tall throughout the rainforest, such as Douglas firs, red cedars, and spruce trees. Popular hiking trails through the forest include the Hall of Mosses Trail and the Hoh River Trail.

MORE TO KNOW

The Hoh Rainforest gets around 140 inches (355.6 cm) of **precipitation** in just one year!

This trail brings visitors through the temperate rainforest in Olympic National Park.

MAGNIFICENT MOUNTAINS

Olympic National Park is home to the Olympic Mountains. The highest one is Mount Olympus. It is 7,980 feet (2,432 m) high.

You can spot snow and ice on the peaks of the mountains. Some Olympic mountains have **glaciers** on them. The biggest glacier is Blue Glacier. It is 2.6 miles (4.2 km) long and about the size of 20 trillion ice cubes! When the glaciers melt, their water flows down to the park's valleys and waterways.

This view shows Mount Olympus, the highest peak in the park.

MORE TO KNOW

Glaciers often leave behind lakes in the mountains. These alpine lakes are an important part of the **ecosystem**.

LIFE IN OLYMPIC

Many different plants and animals live in Olympic National Park. Some live in the surrounding waters, such as dolphins, sea lions, and whales. The lakes and rivers have large numbers of Pacific salmon.

Mountains are home to different species of animals. A few, such as marmots, live up high. Others live in the trees farther down the mountain. Meadows welcome deer, mountain lions, and elk. The wetlands and lowlands are perfect for beavers, salamanders, and frogs.

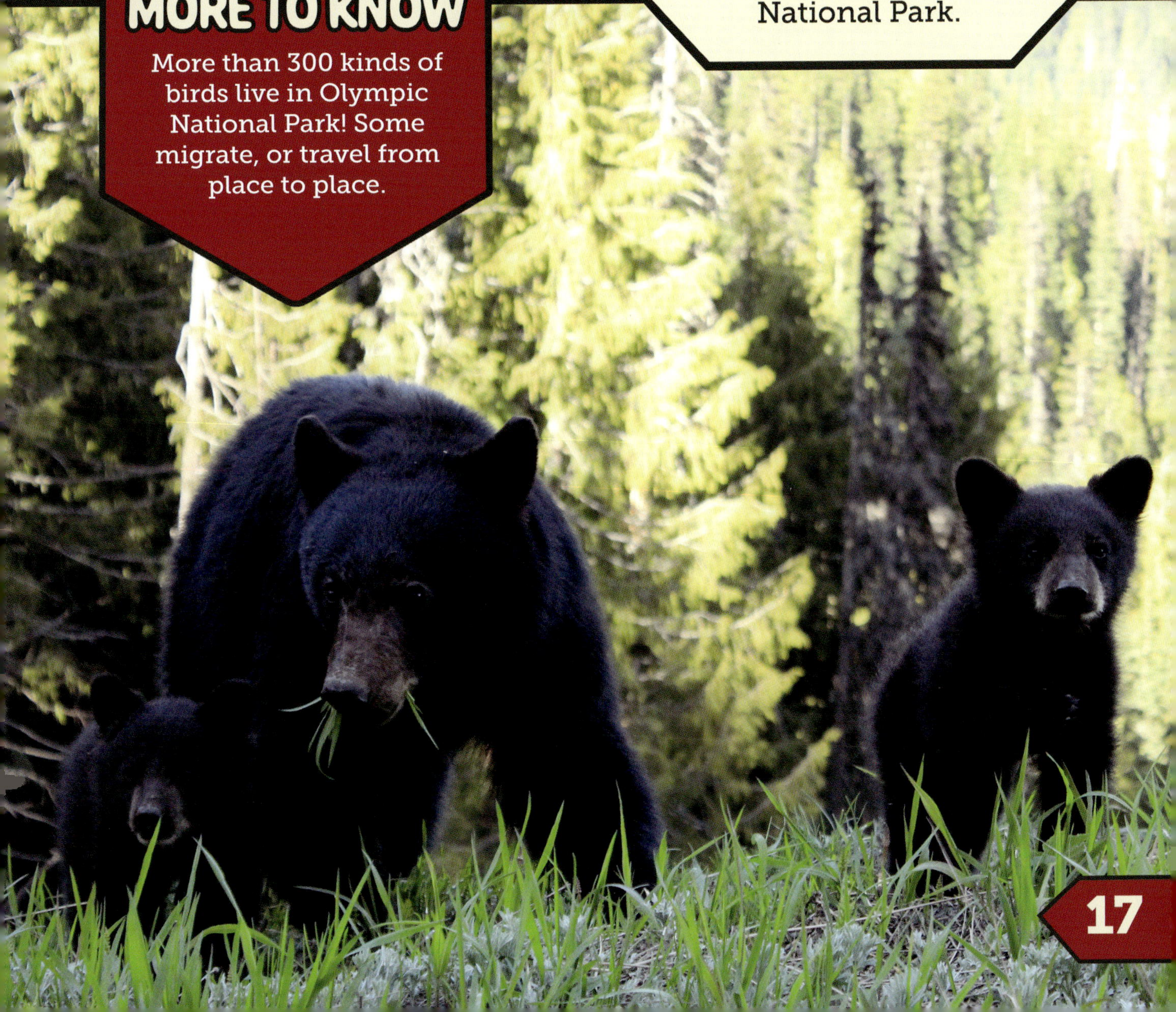

MORE TO KNOW

More than 300 kinds of birds live in Olympic National Park! Some migrate, or travel from place to place.

These black bears live in Olympic National Park.

GET ACTIVE!

There are many ways to explore Olympic National Park. Many people go boating, canoeing, and kayaking in the waters in and around the park. People can also fish there.

Some people hike the forest trails and coastline of Olympic National Park for a day trip. Others hike deep in the wilderness and sleep under the stars. Olympic National Park also has 16 campgrounds for people to stay overnight. Rock climbers can make their way up mountain peaks and glaciers.

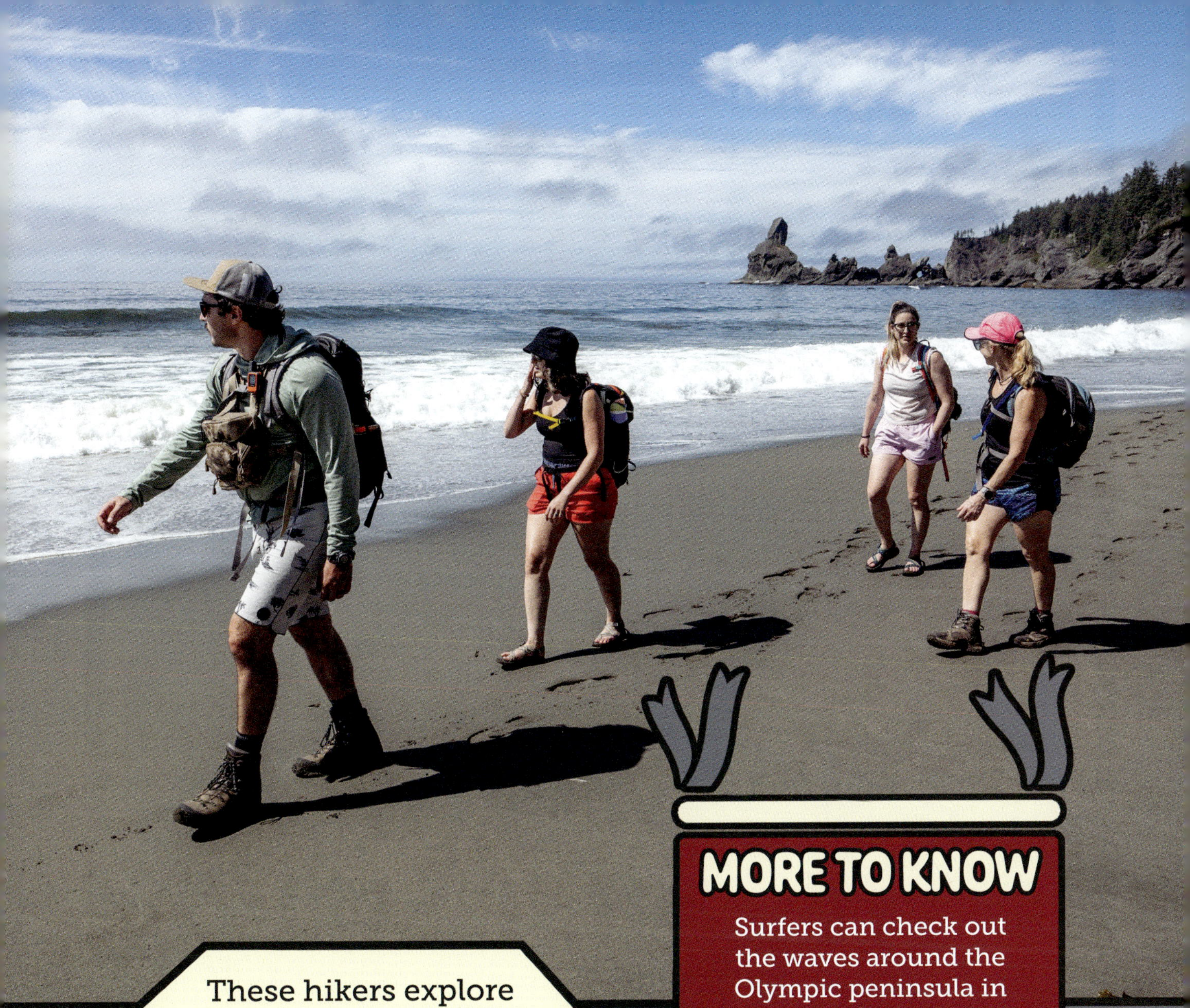

These hikers explore Shi Shi Beach Trail in Olympic National Park.

MORE TO KNOW

Surfers can check out the waves around the Olympic peninsula in areas like La Push and Neah Bay.

PROTECTING THE PACIFIC NORTHWEST

The Pacific Northwest has a landscape and ecosystems that are unlike any others in North America. From mountain peaks to temperate rainforest, this area is a safe space for many species. Some are found nowhere else on Earth!

The government has protected this part of the Pacific Northwest for over a century. Olympic National Park allows animals such as elk, sea otters, and bears to **thrive**. It's important for visitors to respect the land and the animals that call it home.

Olympic National Park protects the one-of-a-kind landscape found in the Pacific Northwest.

MORE TO KNOW

The Olympic marmot is one species that can only be found in Olympic National Park!

OLYMPIC MARMOT

GLOSSARY

attraction: Something people travel to see.

ecosystem: A natural community of life that includes living and nonliving features.

erosion: The act of wearing away by wind or water.

glacier: A large mass of ice formed in cold regions that moves very slowly down a slope or across land.

national monument: A place of historic, scenic, or scientific interest set aside for preservation.

peninsula: A portion of land nearly surrounded by water.

precipitation: Rain, snow, sleet, or hail.

protect: To keep safe.

reserve: An area of public land that is set apart for a purpose.

rugged: Having an uneven surface.

temperate: Having a mild climate that's not too hot or too cold.

thrive: To do well or be successful.

tidepool: A pool of saltwater left by a tide.

FOR MORE INFORMATION

Books

Lawrence, Blythe. *Washington*. Minneapolis, MN: Kids Core, 2025.

Siber, Kate. *National Parks of the U.S.A.* Minneapolis, MN: Wide Eyed Editions, 2024.

Websites

Olympic National Park
kids.britannica.com/kids/article/Olympic-National-Park/489378
Learn more about the geography and history behind Olympic National Park.

Temperate Forest Habitat
kids.nationalgeographic.com/nature/habitats/article/temperate-forest
Discover the amazing features of temperate forest habitats, such as the one found in Olympic National Park.

Publisher's note to educators and parents: Our editors have carefully reviewed these websites to ensure that they are suitable for students. Many websites change frequently, however, and we cannot guarantee that a site's future contents will continue to meet our high standards of quality and educational value. Be advised that students should be closely supervised whenever they access the internet.

INDEX